CONTENTS

ENGINEERING BRITAIN

The Britain that we know today has evolved from centuries of invasions, warfare, farming and industry. The engineering behind buildings, machines and technology has played its part in this history, leaving its mark on the landscape and lifestyle that we have in Britain.

Best of British

Britain has been home to world-leading engineers, inventors, architects and designers who have changed the way Britain and the world works.

Isambard Kingdom Brunel (1806—1859)

Brunel lived during the Industrial Revolution, a time of great change. He designed and built tunnels, bridges, railway lines and ships, making it possible for more people to travel to different parts of the country and the world.

Notable achievements:
- Clifton Suspension Bridge
- Box Tunnel
- SS *Great Eastern*

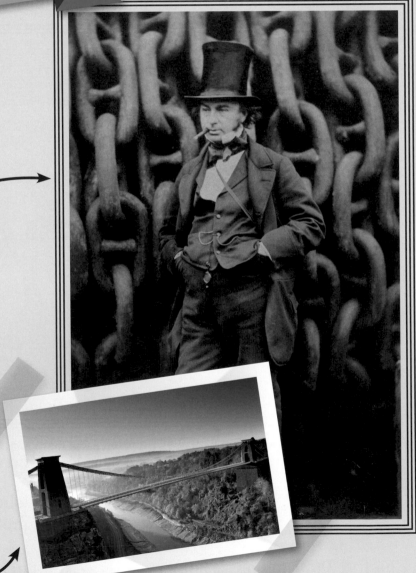

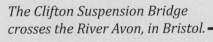

The Clifton Suspension Bridge crosses the River Avon, in Bristol.

British icons

Ada Lovelace (1815–1852)
Scientist and mathematician, considered to be the first computer programmer

Lovelace wrote the first set of instructions for a computer programme before the first computer had even been built.

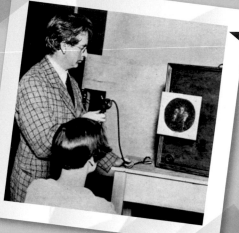

John Logie Baird (1888–1946)
Inventor of the television

John Logie Baird in front of an early television.

Norman Foster (1935—)
Architect of buildings such as Stansted Airport, Wembley Stadium and the Gherkin

The Gherkin opened in 2003 and has fast become an iconic building in London.

Trevor Bayliss (1937—)
Inventor of the wind-up radio

Bayliss invented the wind-up radio so that people in remote places in Africa could have access to information.

The following pages will show feats of engineering that have taken place in Britain or have been created by British innovators. They have all played a part in shaping the history of Britain, creating the world in which we live today.

STONE CIRCLES

Around 5,000 years ago, stone circles were built all over Britain. No one is really sure of their purpose. Some think they were built for ceremonies to worship nature or as a magical place of healing.

Stone circle in Callanish, Outer Hebrides, Scotland

Stonehenge

1

The most impressive stone circle is Stonehenge, in Wiltshire. Its construction is thought to have begun in around 3000 BCE, just before the start of the Bronze Age.

The stones are laid out in a way that suggests it was used as a giant calendar. The entrances towards the circle have been created in line with the direction of the midsummer sunrise and midwinter sunset. When the sun shines directly through the entrances, it marks the changing of the seasons.

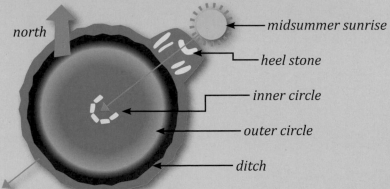

Aerial plan of Stonehenge

north

midsummer sunrise

heel stone

inner circle

outer circle

ditch

midwinter sunset

Moving stones

The large stones that make up Stonehenge came from different parts of the country. It remains a mystery as to how people were able to move the stones. The wheel had yet to arrive in Britain, so they couldn't have used carts or wagons.

The stones from the inner circle come from the Preseli Hills in Wales. One theory is that these stones were dragged over wooden rollers or on a sledge and floated on a raft down the coast and across rivers.

The stones in the outer circle weigh around 50 tonnes each and travelled from Marlborough Downs, Wiltshire. It's been estimated that at least 600 men would have been needed to get one of these stones up a large steep hill on its journey.

Stonehenge

Preseli Hills

Marlborough Downs

Engineering facts

The Iron Age lasted in Britain from 800 BCE to 43 CE. It is so-called as these dates mark the introduction of iron into Britain. Iron is a strong metal that improved the production of tools and weapons. Before iron, people used brittle flint and bone, and a softer metal, bronze.

During the Iron Age there were many Celtic tribes in Britain. They were expert chariot makers and rode into battle on war chariots.

ALL ROADS LEAD TO ROME

When the Romans invaded and settled in Britain, they brought with them a highly disciplined army that could march at least 32 kilometres a day in full armour.

A re-enactor wearing the armour of a Roman soldier.

Straight lines

The army played an important role in maintaining peace across Britain, and were also employed in building the roads upon which they marched up and down the country.

The roads were built in straight lines, which meant that soldiers could march without being ambushed, as there were no corners for people to hide behind. It also meant that they travelled the shortest and most direct route to their destination.

Map showing the network of Roman roads in Britain

● Roman town
Modern-day town

Main Roman roads:
Fosse Way

Watling Street

Ermine Street

Antonine Wall

Hadrian's Wall

Eburacum
York

Mamucium
Manchester

Deva
Chester

Lindum
Lincoln

Venta
Norwich

Venonis
High Cross

Moridunum
Carmarthen

Verulamium
St Albans

Londinium
London

Isca
Exeter

Noviomagus
Chichester

Dubris
Dover

Durnovaria
Dorchester

Many of the Roman roadways have survived. This road, the A5, is built on top of Watling Street.

Roman roads

How to build a Roman road:

1. Dig a ditch at either side of the road area;
2. Pile the soil dug from the ditch into the middle;
3. Place large stones close together on top of the road area;
4. Cover the surface with small stones, stamping them down to fill cracks and smooth the surface.

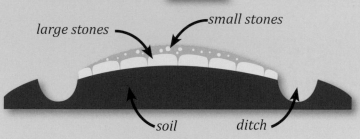

large stones   small stones

soil   ditch

Roman roads were built with a curve in the middle, allowing water to run off into the ditches on either side. This stopped puddles from forming and made the surface last longer.

Engineering facts

The Romans built a system of aqueducts that brought water into towns for fountains, private homes and public baths.
They built tunnels, bridges and pipes that sloped down gently from the water source towards its destination. Traces of aqueducts can be found in St Albans, Chester, Bath, Exeter and York.

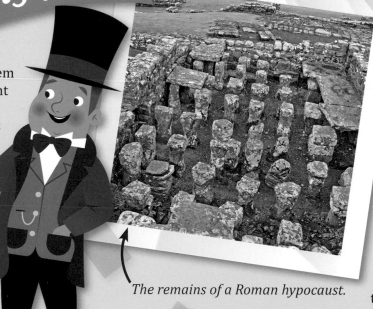

The remains of a Roman hypocaust.

The Romans invented an early form of underfloor heating – the hypocaust. The heat came from a hot furnace that slaves kept alight. The heat moved around the underfloor space of the building, where small columns supported the floor.

Hadrian's Wall was built by the Romans to prevent attacks from tribes in Scotland. It's 117 km long and built over harsh countryside, rivers and crags. It includes ditches, barracks, ramparts and forts, all built within six years.

Hadrian's Wall starts on the east coast at Bowness-on-Sea and crosses over to Newcastle upon Tyne.

FARMING FIELDS

The Anglo-Saxons came to Britain from Germany, Denmark and the Netherlands, settling in kingdoms across the country. Most Anglo-Saxons were farmers and turned areas of land into fields for growing crops.

3

The heavy plough

coulter

This 11th century illustration shows how the heavy plough was used. The coulter is positioned behind the wheel.

The introduction of the heavy plough helped the Anglo-Saxons grow a large amount of food.

The heavy plough contained a metal blade, a coulter, that could dig deep into the ground to turn up fertile soil. This meant that more land could be used for farming, transforming large areas of Britain into a patchwork of fields.

This iron coulter was found by archaeologists in Kent. It dates back to the 7th century.

Marking the land

The heavy plough was used over long narrow strips of ground. It created ridges that can still be seen in some fields today, like here in Leicestershire.

Engineering facts

The Vikings invaded Britain arriving in longships. These boats were built to be light and shallow and could sail across the sea at high speeds. They could also travel in shallow waters and up rivers, surprising people in places where no one expected a ship full of warriors to appear.

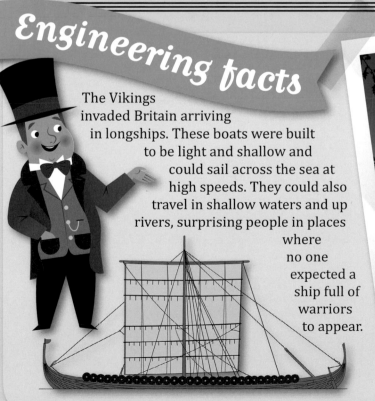

The Anglo-Saxons built many churches across Britain, using local materials. Roofs were largely made of wood, but some were thatched, made from reeds found alongside rivers. Stonework also became more decorative and was often made to look like wood.

The main stonework on the Earls Barton church tower, Northamptonshire, dates from 970. It has been designed to look like timber beams.

CASTLES RULE

When the Normans invaded England they built hundreds of castles across the country. These were built to protect the Norman lords from attacks and were places from where they could govern the local people.

The Norman conquest of England is illustrated in the Bayeux Tapestry. This section shows Norman soldiers building a motte-and-bailey castle.

Motte-and-bailey castles

The type of castles they built are called 'motte-and-bailey castles'. These had a tower on the top of a mound of earth (the motte), surrounded by an enclosure (the bailey) that housed the soldiers and places such as a bakery and a chapel.

Cardiff Castle, built by the Normans, sits on top of a motte.

The Normans first built wooden castles, as these were quick to construct. However, they were also easy for enemies to attack and set on fire. They later built stone castles, and many of these can still be seen in England and Wales today.

Windsor Castle, originally built in the 11th century, has a motte and two baileys.

The White Tower

4

One of the first stone castles the Normans built in England was the White Tower. This is the castle keep, the central and strongest building, that is part of the Tower of London.

Nothing like this had been built in England before. At 27.5 m high, it towered above the wooden buildings of London, giving the same effect as a skyscraper does today.

The Normans constructed 15 large cathedrals across England. Much Norman architecture is characterised by the use of towers. These make the buildings visible from miles around, while also providing high observation points. Their buildings also featured lots of patterned arches.

The original construction took place from around 1075–1100. The White Tower has faced some changes to its appearance over the years, though the original layout remains.

The Tower was an important symbol of Norman power, and has played a significant role in British history ever since. It has been used as a fortress, a royal palace and a prison in which royalty have been kept.

Today it protects the Crown Jewels, a collection of valuable royal treasures that dates back to the 12th century, just after the Norman rule.

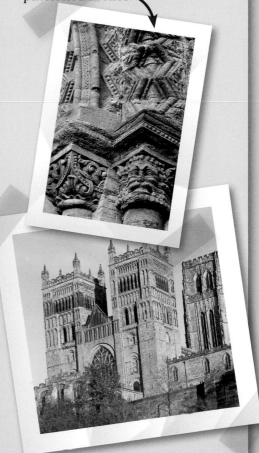

The building of Durham Cathedral began in 1093, and today it still holds much of its original Norman design.

WEAPONS OF WAR

During the Medieval period, Scotland and England fought each other in a series of bloody and brutal wars. The weapons used in battle ranged from swords, axes and longbows to giant siege engines designed to knock down castle walls.

Siege of Stirling Castle

Stirling Castle as it is seen today.

In 1304, King Edward I ordered an attack on Stirling Castle in Scotland. For four months the English army bombarded the castle walls, firing lead and stone missiles from large catapults, called trebuchets.

Frustrated by their slow progress in capturing the castle, Edward got his master craftsmen to build what is thought to be the biggest trebuchet ever constructed – the Warwolf.

Knowledge of the trebuchet came to Britain from France. This illustration, from the end of the 11th century, shows the French army using a trebuchet.

5

The Warwolf

The Warwolf took 50 carpenters three months to build.

It's believed that the sight of the Warwolf was so terrifying that the Scots surrendered before it was used. However, King Edward was so keen to see it in action that he fired it anyway. It lobbed boulders weighing around 136 kg, bringing down a large part of the castle wall.

A reconstruction of the Warwolf at Caerlaverock Castle, Scotland.

Engineering facts

The first recorded appearance of a windmill in Europe is from 1185, in Weedley, a village in Yorkshire. The mills ground corn into flour that was used to bake bread. Windmills made this important part of the British diet more available.

Different versions of a wheelbarrow had been used in ancient Greece and ancient China from as early as 400 BCE. Some had sails and others had the wheel placed in the centre. From the late 12th century the wheelbarrow appeared in England with the wheel at the front.

Reconstruction of a windmill from the Medieval period.

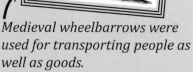

Medieval wheelbarrows were used for transporting people as well as goods.

RULING THE WAVES

During the Tudor period, England faced many attacks from France and Spain, and so building a powerful navy was very important in defending the country.

Battleships

When the Tudor king, Henry VIII, came to power in 1509 he had a fleet of six ships; by the end of his reign, in 1547, England had 57 warships.

Henry transformed the navy. His engineers and ship builders experimented with designs to create large gun ports that allowed his ships to attack from a distance.

King Henry VIII

This 16th century painting, The Embarkation of Henry VIII at Dover, *shows some of Henry's warships.*

The new features pioneered in Tudor warships eventually allowed England, and then Britain, to achieve superiority at sea and build a world-wide empire.

6

The Mary Rose

Henry's most prized ship was the *Mary Rose*. When she was built in 1510 she was the fastest of all the king's ships. In 1536, Henry had her rebuilt, adding gun ports and 91 heavy guns, making her one of the first true battleships.

However in 1545, Henry saw his ship sink. The *Mary Rose* went out to battle carrying 300 more men than usual, many in heavy armour. This extra weight, along with her heavy guns, caused her to tilt, letting water pour in through her open gun ports. She sank before she could fire a shot.

A picture of the Mary Rose *made in the 1540s.*

Engineering facts

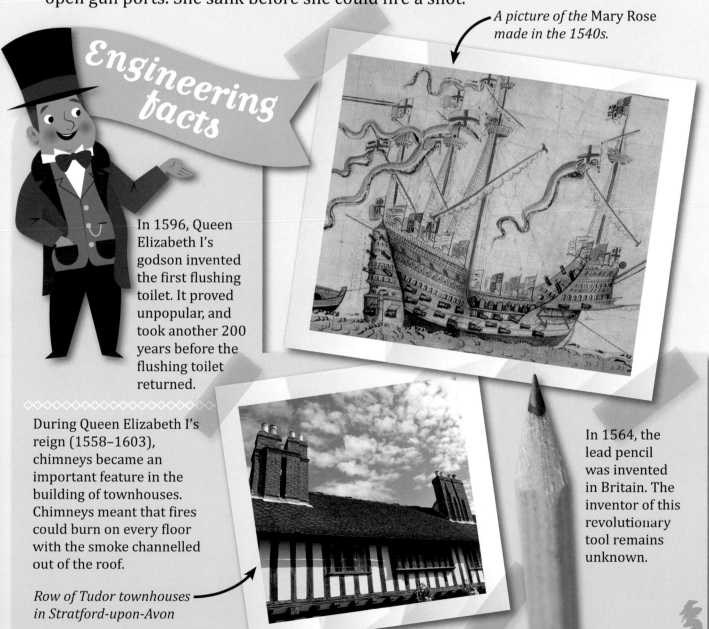

In 1596, Queen Elizabeth I's godson invented the first flushing toilet. It proved unpopular, and took another 200 years before the flushing toilet returned.

During Queen Elizabeth I's reign (1558–1603), chimneys became an important feature in the building of townhouses. Chimneys meant that fires could burn on every floor with the smoke channelled out of the roof.

Row of Tudor townhouses in Stratford-upon-Avon

In 1564, the lead pencil was invented in Britain. The inventor of this revolutionary tool remains unknown.

A FARMING REVOLUTION

Up until the 18th century, methods of farming had not changed for thousands of years. Seeds were planted by hand, a slow process that also caused many seeds to get washed or blown away. Frustrated by this lack of speed and wastage, farmer Jethro Tull invented a machine that transformed farming.

7

The seed drill

Tull set to work building the horse-drawn seed drill, a machine that could drill deep into the soil and plant seeds evenly in rows as it moved along.

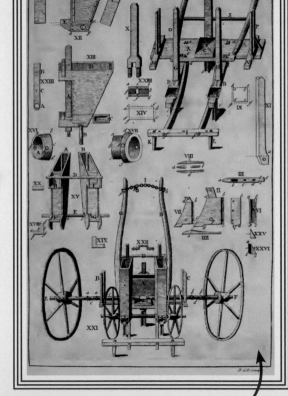

Drawing showing the individual parts that made up Tull's seed drill

Jethro Tull (1674–1741)

At first, people laughed at his machine – he had built his prototype using old foot pedals from his local church organ.

Legacy

Tull went on to prove that using his invention guaranteed the growth of more crops, which also meant that it made the farmer more money.

Tull's machine remains the basis of sowing technology in farming today.

Architect Sir Christopher Wren (1632–1723) was responsible for rebuilding much of London after the Great Fire in 1666. This included 52 churches and St Paul's Cathedral. He built many public buildings across the country that are still standing today.

Modern-day seed drill

Jethro Tull's tombstone, with an engraving of his famous invention

St Paul's Cathedral, London

In 1675, John Ogilby published the first road map of Britain. The ground-breaking atlas, called *Britannia Depicta*, contained the first accurate road maps drawn to help people plan their journeys across the country.

Ogilby's map showing the route from Newmarket, Suffolk to Wells-next-the-Sea, Norfolk

RAILWAY LOCOMOTIVES

The Industrial Revolution began in the 18th century. It was a period when the building of factories and canals and the use of steam engines changed Britain's landscape and economy forever.

Steam power

The Industrial Revolution led to the building of factories that belched out lots of smoke, as shown in this painting from 1801.

Large machinery had depended on horse, water and wind power, but now steam engines could do the job. Moreover, they could do it more quickly and with an increase in productivity.

Steam also powered the new railway locomotives, shortening travel times and connecting towns and people across the country.

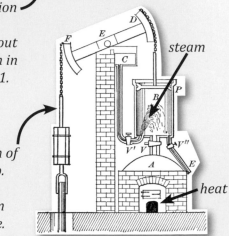

steam

heat

This is an illustration of an early steam pump. It's powered by the compression of steam rising from a furnace.

Stephenson's Rocket

8

Fascinated by the power of steam, British engineer George Stephenson designed what at that time was the fastest machine in the world – a locomotive called *Rocket*.

Rocket was entered into a competition to find the best locomotive that could pull heavy loads over long distances. It was the only locomotive to complete the trial, achieving a record speed of 58 km per hour.

Its success led to the use of *Rocket*-type locomotives on new passenger railways leading to an increase in rail travel up and down the country.

Engineering facts

In 1785, steam was being used to power weaving looms. Looms were used to make cloth and had previously been worked by hand. The steam-powered loom meant that cloth could be woven at a greater speed, but it put the skilled handweaver out of work.

In 1823, Charles Macintosh produced the first waterproof cloth which was then made into a coat – the Macintosh.

In 1827, Edwin Budding invented the first lawn mower. The mower was pushed from behind with rotating blades fixed to the front.

Illustration of an early lawn mower

Modern-day waterproof mac

COMMUNICATION NETWORKS

Huge advances were made in telecommunications during the reign of Queen Victoria. An early form of text messaging appeared in the shape of the telegraph machine, followed 40 years later by the world's first telephone call.

Transport and communication

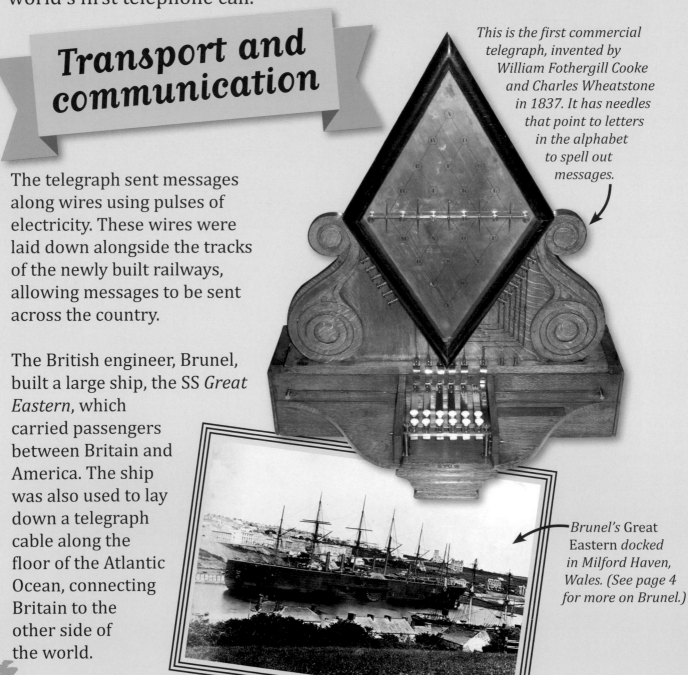

The telegraph sent messages along wires using pulses of electricity. These wires were laid down alongside the tracks of the newly built railways, allowing messages to be sent across the country.

The British engineer, Brunel, built a large ship, the SS *Great Eastern*, which carried passengers between Britain and America. The ship was also used to lay down a telegraph cable along the floor of the Atlantic Ocean, connecting Britain to the other side of the world.

This is the first commercial telegraph, invented by William Fothergill Cooke and Charles Wheatstone in 1837. It has needles that point to letters in the alphabet to spell out messages.

Brunel's Great Eastern *docked in Milford Haven, Wales. (See page 4 for more on Brunel.)*

The telephone

The telegraph spurred on inventors to find a way for the human voice to travel across electrical wires. A breakthrough was made by Edinburgh-born Alexander Graham Bell. On 10 March 1876, he spoke the first words over a telephone wire. They were to his assistant next door, and were, 'Mr Watson, come here, I want to see you.'

By 1879 Britain had its first telephone exchange, allowing people to be connected by telephone across the country. By 1887 there were 26,000 telephones in Britain.

Alexander Graham Bell speaking into an early telephone

Engineering facts

In 1849, Scotsman Kirkpatrick MacMillan invented the first pedal bicycle.

In 1870, James Starley developed the penny-farthing bicycle. It was named after the size of a small and large coin from that time.

In 1863, Britain opened the world's first underground railway line in London.

In 1851, Britain showcased the latest in technology from around the world in the Great Exhibition of the Works of Industry of all Nations. Around 100,000 objects were displayed, with those from Britain filling half of the building. Exhibits included the latest cameras, a printing press and gas cookers.

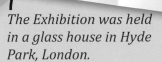

The Exhibition was held in a glass house in Hyde Park, London.

LANDSHIPS

During the First World War (1914–18), vehicles were turned into weapons of war. In the sky, pilots dropped bombs and planes were fitted with machine guns. On the ground, cars were covered with armour and British engineers designed the first tank.

Trench warfare

Both sides at war were engaged in trench warfare. This involved armies firing at each other from opposing trenches, separated by an area known as 'no man's land'. No man's land was thick with mud, and covered with barbed wire and the bodies of dead soldiers who had tried to cross over into enemy lines.

Soldier keeping watch in a trench.

Many cars were adapted with armour and machine guns during the war, but they were not suitable for cross-country travel, as their wheels sank in the mud and their tyres were easily punctured.

An armoured Rolls-Royce stuck in a hole.

The tank

The tank was built to help protect the soldiers as they moved forwards. Originally called a 'landship', it was built with crawler tracks that helped it travel over the churned-up land, and was also fitted with guns to protect its crew.

The tank also became an important war machine during the Second World War (1939–45), with vast improvements made to its speed and firepower.

This is a Mark I tank, the first to be used in battle in 1916.

Engineering facts

John Logie Baird invented the first television, with its public demonstration taking place in 1925. The BBC started broadcasting television programmes from 1932.

In 1914, the Royal Navy launched HMS *Ark Royal*, the first purpose built aircraft carrier. It could carry eight seaplanes and served in both world wars.

The Titanic, *setting sail from Southampton*

RMS *Titanic* was the largest passenger ship at the time it set sail in 1912. It had the luxurious interiors of a top hotel and was thought to be unsinkable. However, on its first voyage it struck an iceberg that tore a hole in the side and caused it to sink. Over half of its passengers died.

In Manchester in 1948, a giant machine, nick-named 'Baby', became the first computer with a memory big enough to run independently a programme from computer code. It had 128 bytes of memory, which is tiny compared to today's computers that have trillions of bytes of memory.

Computer growth

The Baby filled an entire room. It was 5.2 metres in length and 2.24 metres tall. It weighed nearly 1 tonne!

As computing power grew, the size of computers shrank. By the 1980s the computer was portable and cheap enough to appear in the home. Its main use was for data and word processing, and for playing video games.

The ZX Spectrum was a popular British home computer in the 1980s. It was sold as separate pieces of hardware that could be attached to your TV.

The World Wide Web

Tim Berners-Lee

In 1989, British computer scientist, Tim Berners-Lee, invented the World Wide Web (WWW) and revolutionised the way computers are used. The World Wide Web allows us to share and access information for free across all computers.

Today, over 40% of the world's population use the Web. It has changed the world, playing a part in the way we teach and learn, buy and sell, socialise and organise. It is difficult now to imagine a world without the Web.

World Wide Web

The WorldWideWeb (W3) is a wide-area hypermedia information retrieval initiative aiming to give universal access to a large universe of documents.

Everything there is online about W3 is linked directly or indirectly to this document, including an executive summary of the project, Mailing lists , Policy , November's W3 news , Frequently Asked Questions .

What's out there?
    Pointers to the world's online information, subjects , W3 servers, etc.
Help
    on the browser you are using
Software Products
    A list of W3 project components and their current state. (e.g. Line Mode ,X11 Viola , NeXTStep , Servers , Tools , Mail robot , Library)
Technical
    Details of protocols, formats, program internals etc
Bibliography
    Paper documentation on W3 and references.
People
    A list of some people involved in the project.
History
    A summary of the history of the project.
How can I help ?
    If you would like to support the web..
Getting code
    Getting the code by anonymous FTP , etc.

The first web page to go online, posted in 1990. It can be found at: http://info.cern.ch/hypertext/WWW/TheProject.html

Engineering facts

In 1976, Britain, along with France, developed the world's only supersonic passenger aircraft, the Concorde. Its powerful engines meant that a flight from Europe to New York took less than three and a half hours, which is less than half the normal flying time of other planes.

In 1951, the Festival of Britain was held, celebrating Britain's contributions to technology, industrial design and science. It displayed achievements and visions of the future and inspired many up-and-coming engineers and architects.

21st Century
SMARTER PHONES

In 2000, 36% of people in Britain owned a mobile phone and by 2011, this percentage had increased to 76%. Today, there are more mobile phones in Britain than there are people!

Multi-functional

Mobile phone from 2013

Mobile phone from 1983

Mobile phones allow us to be contacted at any time almost anywhere. It's no longer a device you use just to make phone calls, it now plays music, takes pictures and lets you browse the Web – it has become a handheld computer.

The iPhone

British product designer, Jonathan Ive, has crafted iconic gadgets that have changed the way our technology looks and how we interact with it. He is responsible for the design of the iPhone, a phone that pioneered a move away from push-down buttons to touchscreen technology.

Jonathan Ive

Using your fingers to control a product by touching its screen was adapted to the iPad, another Ive design. This led to the rising popularity of tablet computers, and Ive has been called the world's most influential designer.

Engineering facts

The Eden Project is one of the largest botanical gardens in the world. It consists of giant multi-domed greenhouses designed by English architect, Nicholas Grimshaw. These awe-inspiring structures are the largest of their kind, and have been designed so that each dome supports plant life from a different climate around the world.

The Eden Project in Cornwall opened in 2001.

Britain is Europe's largest video game market and leads the world in video game designers.

Further information

Books

Britannia: Great Stories from British History by Geraldine McCaughrean (Orion, 2014)

The Story of Britain by Mick Manning and Brita Granstrom (Franklin Watts, 2014)

Tracking Down series by Moira Butterfield (Franklin Watts, 2013)

The Way Things Work by Neil Ardley (Dorling Kindersley, 2004)

Ways into History: Brunel the Great Engineer by Sally Hewitt (Franklin Watts, 2012)

Websites

BBC Schools site with links to video, photos and facts on the Industrial Revolution in Victorian Britain:
www.bbc.co.uk/schools/primaryhistory/victorian_britain/introduction/

A list of inventions, from A to Z, with links to further information:
www.factmonster.com/science/inventions/inventions-and-discoveries

Listen to a Science Museum (London) curator talk about amazing inventions of the information age:
www.sciencemuseum.org.uk/see-and-do/information-age

Activities and games covering different periods of British history:
www.nationalarchives.gov.uk/education/sessions-and-resources/?resource-type=games

Note to parents and teachers:
Every effort has been made by the publisher to ensure that these websites contain no inappropriate or offensive material. However, because of the nature of the Internet, it is impossible to guarantee that the content of these sites will not be altered. We strongly advise that Internet access is supervised by a responsible adult.

Glossary

aqueduct
a structure with pipes or channels carrying water from one place to another

archaeologist
a person who studies human history through physical remains from the past

Celtic
a description relating to the culture and society of the Celts, a group of people that lived in Britain pre-Roman times

computer code
set of data or instructions in a computer programme

coulter
a blade that is attached to a plough that cuts into the soil

crag
a steep or rugged rock

device
a mechanical object made for a particular purpose

empire
a group of countries governed under a single authority, such as under one ruler or country

estimate
an approximate calculation

fertile
suitable for producing a large number of crops

furnace
a place where heat is generated, usually by fire

gun ports
an opening on the side of a ship through which guns can be fired

hypocaust
a Roman underfloor heating system, with hot air filling hollow space built under floors

icon
a figure held up to great acclaim

Industrial Revolution
a period when society began using machines and factories for producing goods, approximately between 1750–1850

innovator
someone who invents or introduces something new

loom
a tool used for making fabric by weaving together wool or thread

Neolithic
early period of history, also known as the last stage of the Stone Age, when stone tools, pottery and farming developed

pioneer
the first person to do something; leads the way in exploring something new

prototype
the original early version of a design or invention

ramparts
a defensive castle wall with a walkway on top

reign
period of rule by king or queen

siege
to surround and attack a place, often over a long period of time

supersonic
faster than the speed of sound

telecommunication
methods of sending messages electronically

touchscreen technology
machinery controlled by touching a display screen using one or more fingers or a special pen

trebuchet
a large medieval weapon of war used to throw missiles

Index